I0155026

Going Down in a Blip:

The Wreck of the "FOUNTAINHEAD"

By F.M. Starbuck IV

Illustrated by Anna-Maria Guadalupe Ochoa

Going Down in a Blip: The Wreck of the "FOUNTAINHEAD." Copyright © 2020 F.M. Starbuck IV. Produced and printed by Stillwater River Publications. All rights reserved. Written and produced in the United States of America. This book may not be reproduced or sold in any form without the expressed, written permission of the authors and publisher.

Visit our website at **www.StillwaterPress.com** for more information.

Library of Congress Control Number: 2019920794

ISBN: 978-1-950339-72-3

1 2 3 4 5 6 7 8 9 10
Written by F.M. Starbuck IV
Illustrated by Anna-Maria Guadalupe Ochoa
Published by Stillwater River Publications, Pawtucket, RI, USA.

Publisher's Cataloging-In-Publication Data
(Prepared by The Donohue Group, Inc.)

Names: Starbuck, F. M., IV, author. | Ochoa, Anna-Maria Guadalupe, illustrator.
Title: Going down in a blip : the wreck of the Fountainhead / by F.M. Starbuck, IV ; illustrated by
    Anna-Maria Guadalupe Ochoa.
Description: Pawtucket, RI, USA : Stillwater River Publications, [2020]
Identifiers: ISBN 9781950339723
Subjects: LCSH: Rand, Ayn. Fountainhead--Adaptations--Comic books, strips, etc. | Financial services industry--Cor-
    rupt practices--United States--Comic books, strips, etc. | Corporations--Corrupt practices--United States--Comic
    books, strips, etc. | Wall Street (New York, N.Y.)--Moral and ethical aspects--Comic books, strips, etc. | Satire,
    American. | LCGFT: Didactic fiction. | Satirical literature. | Graphic novels.
Classification: LCC PN6727 .S73 2020 PS3537.T3 | DDC 741.5973 813/.52--dc23

The views and opinions expressed in this book are solely those of the author
and do not necessarily reflect the views and opinions of the publisher.

I. NORMAL

FROM HIGH atop the signature Tower—

Way up the drain of command—

—The Chief Extravagant Officer

Pronounces higher quarterly yearnings

Ahead of higher quarterly revisions.

ON COMMAND, the Media Team trumpets:

"GROWTH!"—

—Declares the brand: "BEST IN CLASS!!

MARKET LEADER!!"

Praises the CEO: "CUTTING EDGE!!!

VISIONARY!!! GENIUS!!!"

Tells the world: "THE FUTURE IS OURS!!!!"

UP the down escalator

The Strategic Fanning Division unveils

The same-plan for the upcoming year—

—"WHAT GOES DOWN MUST GO UP!"

"WHAT GOES UP MUST GO UP!"

DOWN the drain of command

A storm in every port—

—Never a full moment—

The harder you work, the harder you fall.

You can't squeeze blood from a phone.

II. PARADIGM SHIFT

SUDDENLY, out of the stew—a news splash!—

—Somewhere, in the sandbars of cyber space

Blows a leak in the hype-line:

A plume of unclean numbers

Escapes into air.

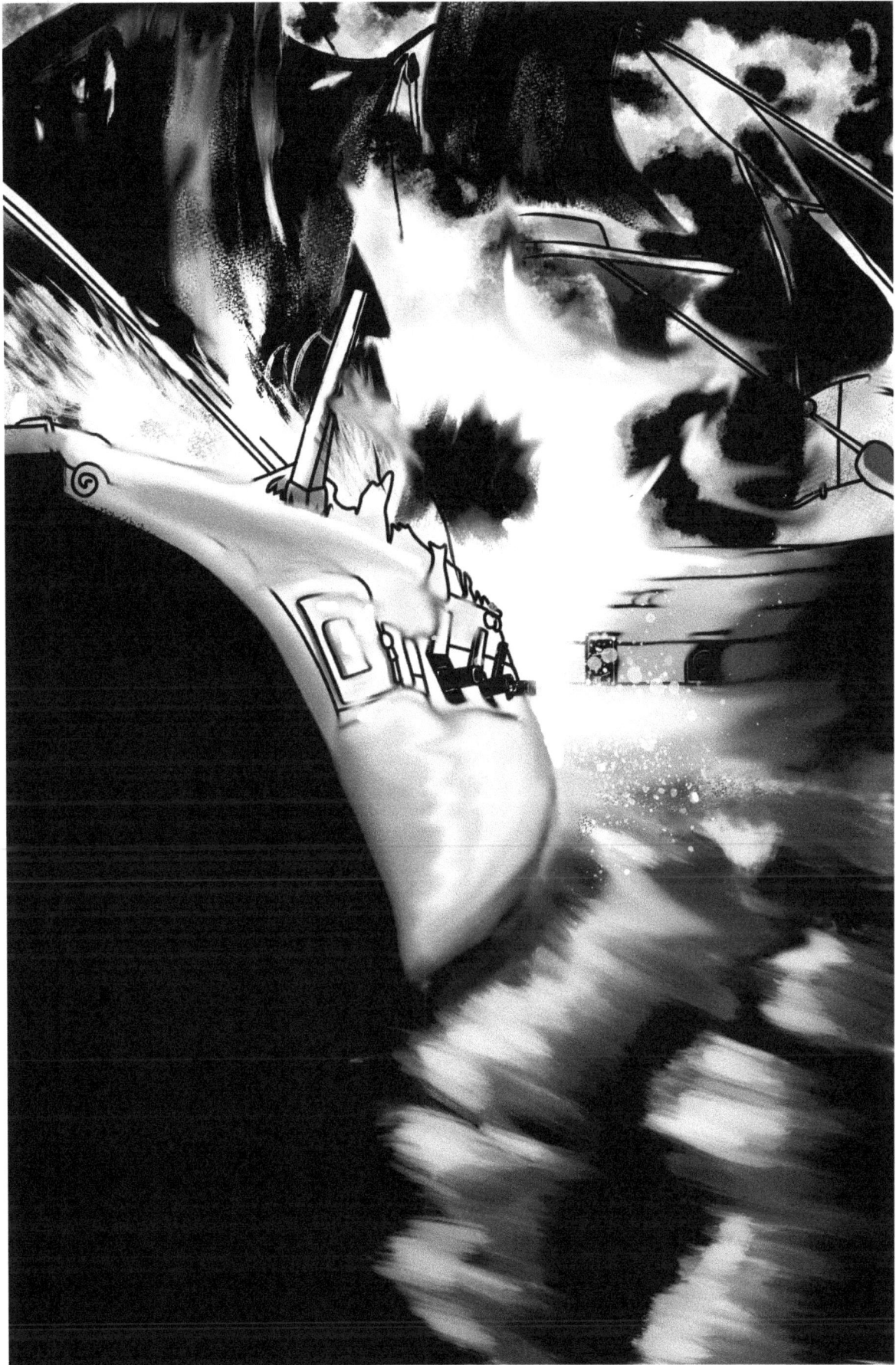

UP and down Wall Streak

The bulls smell mud in the fodder:

SELL YOUR SHORTS!!!!!!—

—Overnight, the company sock

Falls off the hedge.

THE SUMP will come up in the morning.

Viral flows the Dawn!

Water under the dam—

Water over the bridge—

A writhing tide tips all boats!

MASTERS of the marketplace, who knew it all first—

Flood the airwaves with late-breaking ooze:

"THE FAT IS OUT OF THE BAG!"—

—"COOKED THE BOOKS!"

"—THE PARTY'S OVER!"

THERE'S a fright at the end of the funnel!

The brokers run *first* –

Making waves, breaking wind—

—The customer comes *last*—

What goes down must go down.

III. REORGANIZATION

BACK at the tranche,

bunkered down, the CEO intones:

"TAXES!"

"REGULATION!"

"THE ECONOMY!"—

—THE BUCK STOPS OVER *THERE!*"

HIGH atop the glimmering tower

The Legal Team mounts a defense—

—"THE ALLEGATIONS ARE WITHOUT POOF!"

"A CRIMINAL CONSPIRACY TO

RIP OFF OUR SMOCK!"

"SHORT-SMELLERS DRIVEN BY WEED!"

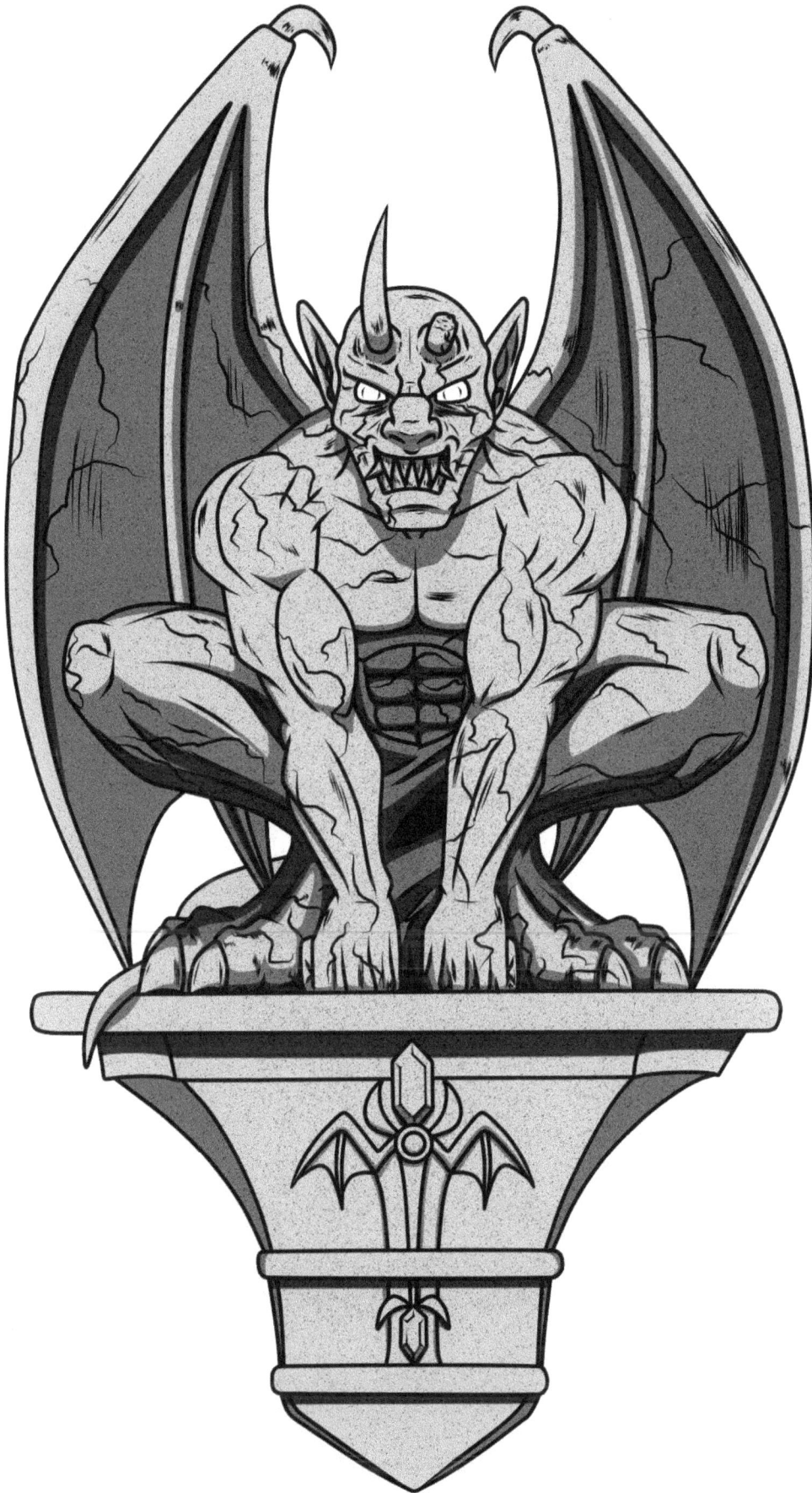

AND the Media Team launches an offense—

—"INTEGRITY—TRANSPARENCY!"

"NO KNOWLEDGE – ROBUST!"

"SHAREHOLDER VALUE!"

"AMERICA!"

FROM deep in the reeds, away up snit creek,

Descends a Management Mask Force,

Inspects every desk and file,

Nabs the ones who did what they're told:

"We've found the smoking bum!"

IV. TRANSITION

BLUE CHIP investors—at the end of their hopes—push back:

"It smells."

On command, Certified Shareholder-enhanced Consultants

Converge on the Expletive Suite

"Nothing under the bums that can't be nixed."

FROM an undisclosed vacation

The Cordon Bleu Board concedes,

"Mini-steaks were made."—

High above earth's orbit,

The awakening Feds respond…

"We'll burn that bridge when we get to it."

CORDON BLEU BOARD willing,

The Strategic Focus Poop concludes—at the end of the pay:

"The Future is hard to Predict"

It's time to slink outside the box.

The ships are leaving the sinking rat.

V. GOLDEN PARACHUTE

THE CEO takes club, stock, office, secretary, condo, and jet,

Perpetual, offshore, tax-free—

—And, running the tab up the flagpole,

Backdates the options.

No barriers to exit!—

Endorsed by the Plaudit Committee.

VI. MERGER

DOWN BELOW: All hands on dreck!

Return your tray tables to their uptight position!

The tie is falling—

—Pressed through proper flannels,

The Human Remorse Department announces

a team-less transition.

It's back to the fault mines.

VII. STREAMLINING

WHEN the going gets tough, the tough take the hit:

Off budget: *EFFECTIVE IMMEDIATELY!*

Down the tubes: *AHEAD OF PLAN!*

Into the drink: *NOTHING PERSONAL!*—

—Straight up with a twist—on the rocks with a splash—

Shaken, not stirred—

Skidding to a halt at the bottom.

VIII. THE BOTTOM LINE

IT'S lonely at the bottom.

IX. THE NEW NORMAL

WAKE up—

Feel the ground.

Breathe deep.

Look around.

—**SMELL** the coffee.

Zip the jeans.

Roll the bedding.

Eat the beans—

—SADDLE UP!

Lock and load.

Move 'em out.

Hit the road.

Tomorrow is another fray.

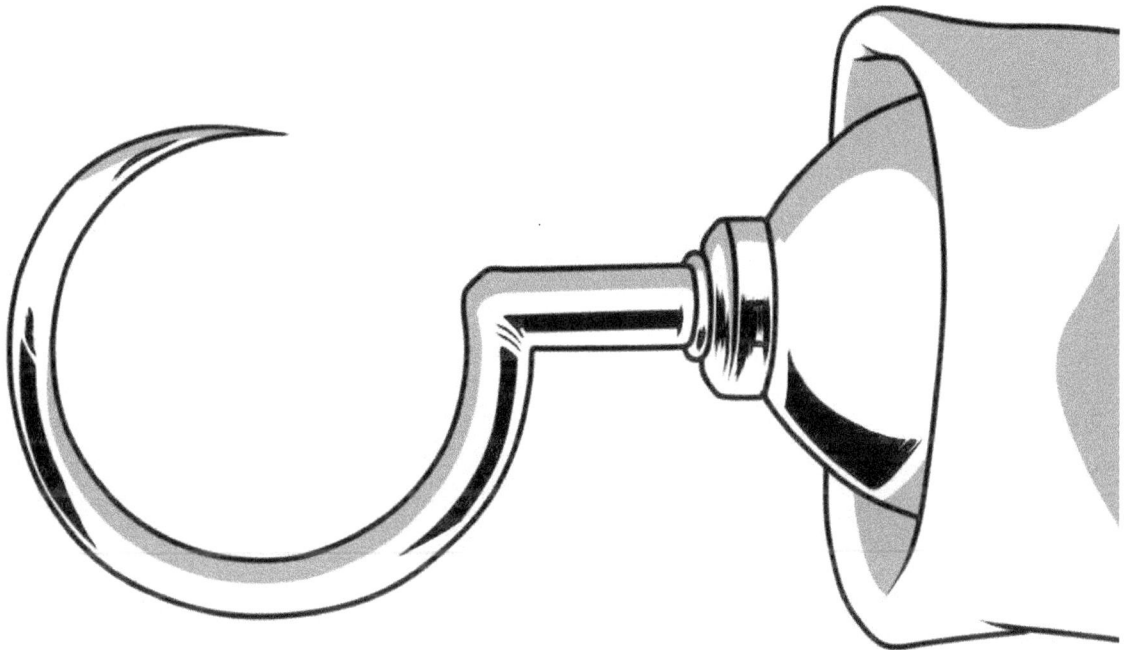

LESSONS LEARNED

"All human wisdom can be summed up in 50 sayings."

THE ORIGINAL SAYINGS

(BEFORE THE WRECK OF THE "FOUNTAINHEAD")

I. NORMAL

The chain of command—
The Chief Executive Officer
Higher quarterly earnings.
Higher quarterly forecasts.

Up the up escalator
The Strategic Planning Division
The gameplan for the upcoming year:
WHAT GOES UP MUST COME DOWN!

The chain of command
A port in every storm.
Never a dull moment
The harder you work, the more you succeed
The bigger they come, the harder they fall.
You can't squeeze blood from a stone.

II. PARADIGM SHIFT

Out of the blue—a news flash!
The vastness of cyber space
Blows a leak in the pipeline—
A plume of poisonous gas

Up and down Wall Street
The bears smell mud in the water:
SELL SHORT!!!!!!
Overnight, the company stock
Falls off the edge.

The sun will come up in the morning.
"Quiet flows the Don!"
Water over the dam—
Water under the bridge—
A rising tide lifts all boats!
Flood the airwaves with late-breaking news:
"THE CAT IS OUT OF THE BAG!"

There's a light at the end of the tunnel!
Making waves / Breaking waves.
The customer comes first—
What goes up must come down.

III. REORGANIZATION

Back at the ranch,
'THE BUCK STOPS HERE!"

"THE ALLEGATIONS ARE WITHOUT PROOF!"
"CRIMINAL CONSPIRACY TO RIP OFF OUR STOCK!"
"SHORT-SELLERS DRIVEN BY GREED!"

From deep in the weeds, away up shit creek,
A Management Task Force,
"We've found the smoking gun."

IV. TRANSITION

Blue Chip investors—at the end of their ropes
Converge on the Executive Suite
"Nothing under the sun that can't be fixed."

From an undisclosed location
The Blue Ribbon Board concedes,
"Mistakes were made."
"We'll cross that bridge when we get to it."

God Willing,
The Strategic Focus Group concludes—at the end of the day:
It's time to think outside the box.
The rats are leaving the sinking ship.

V. GOLDEN PARACHUTE

Running the flag up the flagpole,
Backdates the options.
No barriers to exit!—
Endorsed by the Audit Committee.

VI. MERGER

All hands on deck!
Return your tray tables to their upright position!
The sky is falling.
Pressed through proper channels,
The Human Resource Department announces a seamless transition.
It's back to the salt mines.

VII. STREAMLINING

When the going gets tough, the tough get going:

VIII. THE BOTTOM LINE

It's lonely at the top.

IX. THE NEW NORMAL

Tomorrow is another day.

www.ingramcontent.com/pod-product-compliance
Lightning Source LLC
LaVergne TN
LVHW061335060426
835511LV00014B/1940